ANIMALS

Mice

by Kevin J. Holmes

Content Consultant:
Allison Kaastra
Director of Public Relations
Rat and Mouse Club of America

Bridgestone Books
an imprint of Capstone Press

Bridgestone Books are published by Capstone Press
818 North Willow Street, Mankato, Minnesota 56001
http://www.capstone-press.com

Library of Congress Cataloging-in-Publication Data
Holmes, Kevin J.
　　Mice/by Kevin J. Holmes.
　　　p. cm.--(Animals)
　　Includes bibliographical references and index.
　　Summary: Introduces the world of mice, their physical characteristics, behavior,
and interaction with humans.
　　ISBN 1-56065-604-2
　　1. Mice--Juvenile literature. [1. Mice.] I. Title.
II. Series: Animals (Mankato, Minn.)
QL737.R6H765　1998
599.35--dc21

97-19461
CIP
AC

Photo credits
David Perla, 18
Root Resources/Anthony Merceica, cover, 12
Unicorn Stock/Christian Mundt, 10; Rich Baker, 14; Russel R. Grundke, 16;
　Martha McBride, 20
Visuals Unlimited/William J. Weber, 4, 6, 8

Table of Contents

Ears

Whiskers

Feet

Tail

Fast Facts

Habitat: Mice live in fields and meadows. They also live almost anywhere people do. They live in houses, barns, and other buildings.

Range: Mice live everywhere except Antarctica.

Food: Mice eat grain, nuts, fruit, and seeds. Some eat food crumbs left behind by people. Others eat insects.

Mating: Mice mate up to 17 times per year. There are usually four to nine baby mice in a litter.

Young: Young mice are called kittens. They are born blind and without fur. They leave their mothers two to three weeks after birth.

Mice

Mice are small mammals. A mammal is a warm-blooded animal with a backbone. Warm-blooded means that the animal's body heat stays the same. Its body heat does not change with the outside weather. Mammals also have hair or fur. Young mammals are fed with their mothers' milk.

There are more than 300 kinds of mice. House mice are one of the most common kinds of mice. They are nocturnal. Nocturnal means they are active at night. Mice search for food at night. House mice are also called commensals. Commensals live with humans and eat human food.

Field mice are also common. They live on corn, wheat, and other grains. Mice spread around the world as more people started farming.

There are more than 300 kinds of mice.

What Mice Look Like

Different kinds of mice share many of the same features. They have small, pointed noses and whiskers. Most have black eyes and rounded ears. They have long, scaly tails.

Mice are small animals. They weigh only about one ounce (28 grams). Their heads and bodies are usually three to four inches (seven and one-half to 10 centimeters) long. This does not include their tails. A mouse's tail is almost as long as its body.

Mice have five toes on each of their four feet. Each toe has a sharp claw. The claws help mice grip when they climb.

Mice have two kinds of teeth. Their front teeth are incisors. Incisors are teeth with sharp edges. Mice use them to gnaw on things like wood. Their back teeth are cheek teeth. Cheek teeth are flat. Mice use them for chewing food.

Most mice have black eyes and round ears.

Where Mice Live

The only continent where mice do not live is Antarctica. A continent is a large land mass. Antarctica is too cold for mice.

Mice live in many places. House mice live in homes, barns, and other buildings. Field mice live in meadows, fields, gardens, and swamps.

Mice choose safe places to build nests. Mice begin making paths after they pick a nesting place. These paths run between their nests and their food sources. Mice make nests from soft materials. They use whatever they can find. Often they use leaves, paper, or grass.

Mice stay in one home all their lives. They move only if they have to. Mice move if food runs out. They also move if their homes get too hot or cold.

Mice stay in one home all their lives.

Senses

Mice use their senses to stay alive. They use senses to find food and to avoid danger.

Mice use their ears to sense danger. They hear sounds humans cannot hear. The sounds are too high pitched for human ears. Mice can hear enemies coming long before the enemies arrive.

Mice use their noses to find food and to sense danger. Mice use smell to find their nests. They also use smell to tell each other apart.

Mice use long whiskers to find their way around. Mice do not see well. Their whiskers help them feel things. Whiskers warn mice before they bump into objects. Whiskers also tell mice how big a hole is.

Mice use their whiskers to feel things.

What Mice Eat

Mice eat food crumbs and food people have left uncovered. Mice also eat corn and grain. Some eat fruit, nuts, and seeds. Others eat insects. Mice will eat almost anything.

Some mice must eat their weight in food every day. They must be active day and night to find enough food. They do not sleep for long periods. Instead, they take many short naps.

Mice eat more than usual in fall. This is when there is a lot of food around. They store food in burrows and other hiding places. A burrow is a hole made by an animal as a home. Stored food is called a hoard. Mice save hoards for winter when food is harder to find.

Mice will eat almost anything.

Enemies of Mice

Mice have many enemies. Many animals hunt and eat mice. Mice also face many dangers. Cold weather, hunger, and illness can harm mice.

People are one of the greatest dangers mice face. Many people try to trap and poison mice.

Mice have other enemies in fields, woodlands, and swamps. Weasels, birds, foxes, snakes, and owls kill mice.

Mice are small and cannot fight back. They can only run away. Mice run in zigzag patterns when trying to escape. This makes them harder to catch.

Snakes kill mice for food.

Young Mice

Mice mate up to 17 times each year. Mating is joining together to produce young. A female mouse has four to nine kittens in each litter. Young mice are called kittens. A litter is a family of animals born at the same time.

Kittens are born without hair. Most kittens are pink, but some are darker colors. They cannot see. They rely on their mothers for food. Kittens cannot leave the nest.

Kittens grow quickly. Some kittens grow fur after just four days. Field mice leave their mothers when they are two weeks old. House mice take longer to grow. House mice leave the nest when they are three weeks old.

Mice find their own places to live after leaving a nest. They build their own nests. Mice mark their nests with urine. This tells other mice to stay away.

Kittens grow quickly.

Mice and People

Some mice cause problems for humans. They eat human food. They sometimes carry illnesses that are dangerous to people. If left alone, mice can increase in numbers quickly. People often try to control mice with traps and poisons.

Mice can also help people. Scientists study some mice. The scientists hope to find cures for sicknesses.

Some mice make good pets. These are not regular house mice or field mice. Special kinds of mice are kept as pets.

Pet mice are easy to care for. They do not need much attention. Pet mice are playful and active. They run, jump, and groom each other. Groom means to clean. Some mice learn to eat out of their owners' hands. Mice will even sit on their owners' shoulders.

Some mice are kept as pets.

Hands On: Touch Test

Humans first sense the world with their eyes. Many animals use other senses first. Mice use hearing and feeling. This activity helps you understand how mice sense the world.

What You Need

12 objects
Handkerchief

What You Do

1. Ask a friend to join you for this activity.
2. Find six different objects each. Any object that fits in your hands will work. Do not show each other your objects.
3. Use the handkerchief as a blindfold to cover your friend's eyes.
4. Place objects one at a time in your friend's hands. Ask your friend to guess what each object is. Give one point for each correct guess.
5. Take turns guessing. Compare your point totals.

Words to Know

cheek teeth (CHEEK TEETH)—back teeth mice use for chewing

commensals (kuh-MEN-sals)—animals that share living space and food with humans

hoard (HORD)—food gathered together and stored in piles

incisors (in-SIZE-ors)—long, sharp front teeth used for gnawing

kitten (KIT-uhn)—a young mouse

litter (LIT-ur)—a family of animals born at the same time

Read More

Harrison, Virginia. *The World of Mice*. Milwaukee: Gareth Stevens Children's Books, 1988.

Horner, Susan. *Nature's Children: Mice*. Danbury, Conn.: Grolier, 1986.

Useful Addresses

American Society for the Prevention of Cruelty to Animals (ASPCA)
424 East 92nd Street
New York, NY 10128-6804

Rat and Mouse Club of America (RMCA)
13075 Springdale Street
Suite 302
Westminster, CA 92683

Internet Sites

The House of Mouse
http://www.perfect.com/mouse/

Rat and Mouse Club of America
http://www.rmca.org/

Index